BUSINESS GROWTH AND DEVELOPMENT IDEAS FOR SENIORS

STEP BY STEP PRINCIPLES LEADING ENTERPRENURES USED FOR CAREER SUCCESS

David C. Thorpe

INTRODUCTION

Navigating The Landscape of Senior Leadership In Business Growth

In the dynamic landscape of today's business world, senior leaders find themselves at the nexus of experience and innovation, shouldering the responsibility of steering their organizations through an ever-evolving terrain. The challenges you face are unique: the need for strategic foresight, adaptability to change, and the relentless pursuit of sustainable growth.

As seasoned professionals, your journey has been marked by success, but it's also punctuated by the complexities of a rapidly changing market.

Have you ever found yourself at the crossroads of tradition and innovation, wondering how to bridge the gap? Are you seeking a comprehensive solution to the intricacies of strategic planning and talent management in an era where the only constant is change?

For many senior leaders, the path to growth and development is riddled with challenges. The relentless pace of technological evolution, the demand for continuous innovation, and the shifting sands of customer expectations create a landscape that requires not just experience but strategic acumen. It's a balancing act between preserving the legacy of the past and pioneering the future.

How do you navigate the complexities of this digital age while ensuring that your organization remains not only relevant but ahead of the curve? How do you foster innovation without compromising the stability of financial foundations? These questions resonate with the pain points you grapple with on a daily basis.

The Benefits of Reading

Enter "Business Growth and Development for Seniors." This book is more than just a guide; it's a strategic companion crafted with you in mind. Within these pages, you'll discover eleven essential steps that serve as a roadmap for propelling your organization to new heights. This isn't just theoretical; these are battle-tested strategies born out of real-world experiences and industry best practices.

Uncover the secrets of effective strategic planning, where we delve into not just setting goals but aligning them with the very fabric of your organization's DNA. Dive deep into market intelligence, gaining insights into not just market trends but also understanding the dynamics of competition and identifying opportunities where others might see challenges.

Your Solution Unveiled

This book is your solution to the challenges that accompany leadership in an era of unprecedented change. It's a toolkit for enhancing customer satisfaction, a manual for fostering a culture of innovation, and a guidebook for managing talent in a way that ensures both continuity and evolution.

 Learn the art of financial management that goes beyond the balance sheet, ensuring a robust financial foundation that propels growth rather than stifling it.

But it doesn't end there. "Business Growth and Development for Seniors" is an invitation to explore the uncharted territory of strategic partnerships and alliances—a terrain where mutual growth becomes not just a goal but a reality.

Are you ready to redefine your leadership, elevate your organization, and thrive in today's dynamic business landscape? "Business Growth and Development for Seniors" is not just a book; it's your key to unlocking the doors of success in the world of business, where the only constant is change.

CHAPTER 1

Foundation and Outline

In the consistently developing scene of business, senior pioneers wind up in charge of associations that should explore complicated and dynamic territory. The Foundation and Outline segment of this guide plans to set the stage by recognizing the remarkable difficulties faced by pioneers in the present high-speed climate.

This section honors the rich history of senior leaders' journeys and the lessons they have learned along the way, recognizing the extensive experience they bring to the table. It dives into the development of business scenes, featuring the groundbreaking minutes that have formed the present.

By establishing the perusal in this verifiable setting, we expect to cultivate a profound comprehension of the establishments whereupon the aid is fabricated.

Significance of Business Development and Advancement

The significance of business development and advancement couldn't possibly be more significant. The significance of these two interconnected aspects in the context of organizational success is outlined in this section. Business development isn't simply a mathematical increment; it addresses the association's capacity to flourish, adjust, and improve because of outside and inward upgrades.

We dive into the ramifications of stale development and the possible ramifications for an association. Whether it's jumping all over market chances, remaining in front of contenders, or drawing in top talent, the significance of development and improvement penetrates each feature of a fruitful business technique. By enlightening the basic role these viewpoints play, this guide tries to impart a need to get moving and reason in the personalities of senior pioneers.

Goals of the Aide

As senior pioneers set out on the excursion illustrated in this aide, lucidity on the targets becomes foremost. This part expresses the aide's motivation: to give an exhaustive guide to accomplishing economical business development and improvement. It means to furnish pioneers with the information, methodologies, and instruments expected to explore the difficulties of the contemporary business scene.

The aide's essential goal is to engage senior pioneers with noteworthy experiences, cultivate a proactive mentality, and impart trust in direction. It wants to be more than just a theoretical discussion; it wants to provide real-world-based, practical solutions. Readers should have a clear understanding of what to anticipate and the transformative potential of the subsequent chapters by the time this chapter concludes.

CHAPTER 2

Key Preparation

2.1 Characterizing a Thorough Business Methodology

In the unpredictable dance of business, an obvious system is the movement that directs each move. Characterizing a Thorough Business Methodology is the foundation of this part, underscoring the significance of clarity and prescience in charting the course for hierarchical achievement.

The traditional method of strategic planning is not the only one covered in this section. It encourages senior leaders to weave a narrative that is consistent with the organization's values, vision, and market positioning, in addition to setting goals. By characterizing a methodology that incorporates both transient successes and long-term desires, pioneers can make a guide that adjusts to the unique ideas of the business scene.

2.2 Adjusting Procedures to Authoritative Objectives

A procedure, regardless of how well it is created, is only successful when it flawlessly lines up with hierarchical objectives. This segment digs into the perplexing system of guaranteeing that each feature of the methodology reverberates with the overall goals of the association.

The arrangement isn't just about rationality on paper; it's about making a collaboration that saturates the hierarchical culture.

Senior pioneers will investigate techniques to flow key needs all through the association, guaranteeing that each colleague grasps their job in the bigger picture. Through genuine models and pragmatic experiences, this part shows the extraordinary force of vital arrangement in driving aggregate endeavors towards a typical vision.

2.3 Distinguishing Key Execution Markers (KPIs)

In the domain of vital preparation, achievement isn't simply estimated by the completion of undertakings; it's checked from the perspective of Key Execution Pointers (KPIs). This part demystifies the method involved with distinguishing KPIs, stressing their job as the compass that guides navigation and execution assessment.

Perusers will investigate the specialty of choosing KPIs that are quantitative as well as intelligent of the association's essential targets. From monetary measurements to consumer loyalty files, this segment gives a thorough manual for picking KPIs that line up with the one-of-a kind objectives of every association. By and by, senior pioneers will comprehend how these pointers act as indispensable signs, guiding the association toward progress, and why it is important to flag when the course redresses.

CHAPTER 3

3.1 Leading Compelling Statistical surveying

In the maze of business development, a successful route starts with a significant comprehension of the territory. Leading Compelling Statistical Surveying is the bedrock of this part, highlighting the basic job of data in pursuing informed vital choices.

This section delves deeper into the intricacies of gathering insights that can be put into action than just the surface level of market research. Customer interviews, trend analysis, and data-driven approaches are all examples of methods that go beyond conventional surveys.

The dynamic nature of markets and the requirement for ongoing, adaptable research to stay ahead of the curve will become more apparent to senior leaders.

3.2 Adjusting to Industry Patterns

The business scene is a continually developing biological system, with industry patterns filling in as a gauge of progress. This segment highlights the significance of recognizing patterns as well as embracing them as impetuses for advancement and development.

Senior pioneers will investigate techniques for expecting shifts in shopper conduct, arising advances, and worldwide market elements. Accentuation is put on the specialty of proactive transformation, where associations move past simple endurance to flourishing amidst change. Certifiable models will delineate how organizations have effectively outfit patterns for their potential benefit, filling in as motivation for pioneers looking to situate their associations at the front of their enterprises.

3.3 Keeping an Eye on Competitors and Looking for Opportunities. In the fiercely competitive business world, knowledge is power, so keeping an eye on competitors is a strategic necessity. This section delves into the art of deciphering the strategies of competitors, identifying their strengths and weaknesses, and utilizing this intelligence to identify opportunities that have not been taken advantage of.

Senior pioneers will figure out how to build a thorough, serious examination system, going past superficial perceptions. The attention is on figuring out the 'why' behind contenders' activities and utilizing this information to tweak hierarchical procedures.

This section provides leaders with the tools they need to not only respond to rivals but also actively shape their own path in the market through case studies and practical insights.

CHAPTER 4

Client-Driven Approach

4.1 Focusing on Consumer loyalty

In the domain of business development, the compass that guides associations toward practical achievement is unquestionably consumer loyalty. Focusing on consumer loyalty is the basic rule of this section, highlighting the significant effect that blissful and faithful clients can have on an association's primary concern.

This segment investigates the all-encompassing perspective on consumer loyalty, stretching beyond the conventional thoughts of item quality and administration proficiency. It examines the emotional aspects of customer interactions and stresses the significance of cultivating relationships that transcend transactional exchanges. Certifiable contextual investigations will enlighten the groundbreaking force of client centricity, showing how associations that focus on fulfillment encourage brand dependability and support.

4.2 Incorporating Customer Feedback. In today's ever-changing business environment, the customer's voice is an invaluable resource. Consolidating client criticism turns into an essential basic in this part, as senior pioneers find the undiscovered abundance of bits of knowledge implanted in client feelings and encounters.

This segment frames procedures for gathering, examining, and following up on client criticism. It stresses the requirement for associations to develop an input-accommodating society where clients feel engaged to straightforwardly share their considerations. Through commonsense tips and examples of overcoming adversity, senior pioneers will figure out how to transform client input into an impetus for consistent improvement, development, and eventually, upgraded consumer loyalty.

4.3 Adjusting Items and Administrations to Client Needs

Items and administrations that reverberate with client needs are the backbone of a client-driven association. Adjusting Items and Administrations to Client Needs is the perfection of an essential methodology that pays attention to clients as well as effectively answers their developing inclinations and assumptions.

This segment investigates the iterative course of adjusting contributions in view of client bits of knowledge, market drifts, and arising advancements. Senior pioneers will acquire experience in the sensitive balance between remaining consistent with authoritative character and deftly acclimating to fulfill client needs. True models will demonstrate how associations that focus on variation witness expanded consumer loyalty as well as an upper hand in a steadily evolving market.

CHAPTER 5

5.1 Encouraging a Culture of Development

In the powerful world of business, the capacity to develop isn't simply an upper hand; there is a need for supportable development. Encouraging a Culture of Development is the foundation of this part, underscoring that development isn't the sole liability of research and development divisions but rather an aggregate ethos that penetrates each feature of an association.

This segment investigates the attitudes and ways of behaving that portray creative societies. It delves into the role that leadership plays in encouraging calculated risk-taking, promoting a sense of curiosity, and championing innovation. Senior executives will learn from real-world case studies how companies that build innovation into their

DNA not only respond to problems well but also actively shape their industries' future.

5.2 Putting resources into Innovative work

Chasing a lively development culture, interest in innovative work arises as an essential support point. This segment enlightens the basic job of research and development in driving authoritative development, exhibiting that interests in investigating the obscure can yield extraordinary results.

Senior pioneers will investigate philosophies for adjusting research and development drives to all-encompassing business procedures. The segment underlines the requirement for a harmony between transient increases and long-haul developments, giving bits of knowledge into compelling spending plan distribution and hazarding the executives. Through commonsense experiences, pioneers will comprehend how vital research and development speculations drive item and administration advancement, yet additionally position associations as industry pioneers.

5.3 Remaining In front of the Opposition

Development isn't just about ideation; it's about reliably dominating the opposition. The culmination of an innovation-focused strategy is "Staying Ahead of the Competition," which emphasizes the symbiotic relationship between innovation and a long-term competitive advantage.

This part investigates the systems associations utilize to remain at the very forefront of their enterprises. Senior leaders will discover the proactive measures that ensure their organizations are not only keeping pace but also setting the pace, such as utilizing emerging technologies and anticipating market trends. Certifiable models will understand that remaining ahead in the development game isn't just about endurance; it's about driving and impacting the direction of the market.

CHAPTER 6

6.1 Drawing in and Holding Top Ability

In the serious world of business, an association's prosperity is unpredictably attached to the type of its ability. Drawing in and holding top ability isn't simply a HR basic, but an essential need for supported development and improvement.

This part dives into the diverse methodology expected to establish a climate where top-level ability isn't simply attracted to your association but is constrained to remain.

To draw in the best, this part stresses the significance of developing a convincing business brand. It investigates procedures to exhibit the association's way of life, values, and obligation to proficiently turn events. The part additionally digs into the job of cutthroat remuneration, advantages, and balance between fun and serious activities in the enlistment cycle.

Maintenance methodologies are similarly essential, with an emphasis on establishing a positive workplace that encourages representative commitment and dependability. Senior pioneers will acquire experiences in building a culture of nonstop learning and giving roads to professional success.

Certifiable models will show how associations that focus on drawing in and holding top ability are better situated to develop, adjust, and make supported progress.

6.2 Administration Improvement for Hierarchical Congruity

The heartbeat of an association lies in its administration. Initiative Improvement for Hierarchical Congruity isn't just about prepping a couple of highly likely people; it's tied in with cultivating a culture where administration is an aggregate liability that guarantees congruity, strength, and flexibility. This part investigates the basic parts of administration advancement programs that go past oddball studios to make an enduring authoritative effect.

The part starts by characterizing the initiative characteristics expected for the association's future vision. It emphasizes the significance of cultivating a diverse leadership pipeline by identifying leadership potential at all organizational levels. Systems for mentorship and instructing are investigated, exhibiting the way that carefully prepared pioneers can direct arising abilities.

The segment further dives into the job of experiential getting the hang of, furnishing pioneers with certifiable provokes and chances to apply and upgrade their abilities. It features the value of constant criticism and execution evaluations in forming pioneers who can explore the intricacies of the business scene.

Through contextual investigations and useful bits of knowledge, senior pioneers will figure out how viable initiative improvement contributes not exclusively to the development of individual pioneers but also to the versatility and progression of the whole association. It exhibits that an advanced authority pipeline is an essential resource that guarantees hierarchical versatility and progress despite developing difficulties.

CHAPTER 7

Monetary Wellness

7.1 Judicious Monetary Administration

In the steadily changing world of business, the capacity to explore the monetary landscape with discernment is vital. Judicious Monetary Administration remains at the center of this section, underscoring the significance of key monetary decision-making and production for hierarchical achievement.

This segment dives into the standards of monetary stewardship that go beyond simple planning, underscoring the job of money as an essential accomplice in driving development.

The part starts by illustrating the essentials of monetary administration, from making hearty monetary designs to adjusting them to overall business systems. It investigates the significance of chance administration and possibility arranging, guaranteeing that associations are versatile even with monetary vulnerabilities. Genuine contextual investigations will outline how associations that focus on reasonable monetary administration climate monetary tempests as well as arise more grounded and more spry.

7.2 Ensuring Healthy Cash Flow. Cash flow is any business's lifeblood, and ensuring healthy cash flow is a crucial part of being financially healthy. The intricacies of cash flow management are discussed in depth in this section, with an emphasis on its role in sustaining day-to-day operations and facilitating strategic initiatives.

Senior pioneers will investigate methodologies to streamline working capital, diminish installment cycles, and oversee receivables. The part likewise addresses the significance of keeping a balance between putting resources into useful learning experiences and saving money for unanticipated conditions.

Through commonsense experiences, pioneers will acquire a comprehension of how a proactive way to deal with income for executives can be an impetus for immediately jumping all over market chances and guaranteeing hierarchical steadiness.

7.3 Expense Enhancement and Productivity Upgrades

Chasing after monetary wellness, associations should investigate expenses and embrace constant effectiveness enhancements. The final piece of the financial fitness puzzle is cost optimization and efficiency enhancements, which demonstrate how organizations can maintain a lean operational structure without compromising innovation or productivity.

In order to foster a culture of cost-consciousness throughout the organization, this section examines methods for locating and eliminating inefficiencies in processes. It accentuates the job of innovation in smoothing out tasks and diminishing overheads.

Certifiable models will exhibit how associations that focus on cost streamlining climate monetary slumps all the more successfully as well as position themselves for supported development.

The section likewise addresses the fragile harmony between cost-cutting measures and encouraging a culture of development. It features how key interests in innovation and representative improvement can prompt long-haul proficiency gains and practical expense for executives.

Through a complete investigation of judicious monetary administration, sound income practices, and cost improvement methodologies, senior pioneers will be furnished with the information and instruments to guarantee the monetary wellness of their associations. This section intends to engage pioneers to make informed monetary choices that add to the drawn-out progress and versatility of their organizations

CHAPTER 8

Associations and Coalitions

8.1 Investigating Key Organizations

In the complex embroidery of business development, vital organizations arise as strong impetuses for advancement, extension, and shared accomplishment. Investigating vital associations is the foundation of this part, stressing the extraordinary potential that emerges when associations work together in an intelligent way.

This segment starts by characterizing the substance of vital associations, moving past customary joint efforts to investigate imaginative models that line up with the drawn-out objectives of the two players. It tends to be the model for choosing reasonable accomplices, underscoring shared values, integral qualities, and a common obligation to progress.

Through true contextual investigations, senior pioneers will acquire bits of knowledge into the substantial advantages of key organizations, from shared assets and hazard moderation to sped up item advancement and admittance to new business sectors.

In addition, the section discusses how effective collaboration, trust-building, and clear communication are crucial to maximizing the value of strategic partnerships.

8.2 Working together for Shared Development

Cooperation isn't simply a popular expression; a powerful power drives associations forward. Teaming up for shared development frames the core of this segment, investigating the harmonious connections that lead to aggregate achievement and supported development.

The part digs into the complexities of encouraging a cooperative culture inside and past hierarchical limits. It looks at ways to break down silos, encourage cross-functional collaboration, and use different points of view to come up with creative solutions to problems. Genuine models will show how associations that focus on cooperation improve their inward capacities as well as make an organization of partners that impel them toward shared targets.

The part likewise addresses the difficulties and arrangements related to cooperative undertakings, featuring the significance of powerful correspondence, trust-building, and a common vision for shared development. Strategies for resolving conflicts, navigating complexities, and ensuring that collaborative efforts contribute to the overarching goals of both parties will be revealed to leaders.

8.3 Getting to New Business sectors and Innovations

In a time of globalization and fast mechanical progression, the capacity to get to new business sectors and advancements can be a distinct advantage for associations. Getting to New Business Sectors and Advancements is the last boondock of this section, showing how key associations and coalitions can be doors to undiscovered open doors.

In this section, we look at how partnerships can help businesses reach new markets, reach new customer types, and expand geographically. It likewise digs into the potential for innovation, trade, and co-development, underscoring how partnerships can give associations an upper hand through shared mastery and access to state-of-the art advancements.

Through viable bits of knowledge and contextual analyses, senior pioneers will comprehend the essential contemplations associated with exploring organizations for market and innovative development. In order to realize the full potential of new technologies and markets, this section emphasizes the need for a forward-thinking approach, adaptability to change, and a commitment to ongoing collaboration.

CONCLUSION

A Journey to Unprecedented Growth and Excellence As this comprehensive guide to business growth and development comes to an end, we take stock of the transformative journey we've taken together. We've explored the complicated scene of vital preparation, market knowledge, client centricity, advancement culture, ability of executives, monetary wellness, and key associations. Every section has been a stepping stone toward exceptional development and greatness in the unique universe of business.

This guide was written with senior leaders in mind—those who not only bear the weight of organizational responsibilities but also have the power to determine their businesses' future. Our investigation started by recognizing the verifiable woven artwork that shapes the present business difficulties and amazing open doors. We perceived the rich encounters and examples mastered, establishing the groundwork for a ground-breaking approach.

Vital Arranging arose as the compass, directing pioneers to characterize exhaustive business procedures, adjust them to authoritative objectives, and recognize key execution markers.

The significance of lucidity, flexibility, and a forward-looking point of view were enlightened, laying the foundation for a key guide that stands tough notwithstanding change.

Market insight turned into the craft of expectation, with powerful statistical surveying, transformation to industry patterns, and careful contender checking filling in as instruments for informed navigation. The capacity to peruse the market beat and distinguish open doors in the midst of difficulties arose as a sign of effective senior administration.

A client-driven approach turned into the heartbeat of reasonable development, with an accent on focusing on consumer loyalty, consolidating input, and adjusting items and administrations to meet advancing client needs. We perceived that client unwaveringness isn't simply a metric but rather a demonstration of an association's obligation to greatness and responsiveness.

Development culture turned into the main thrust for associations, pointing not exclusively to make due yet to flourish. Organizations at the cutting edge of progress now rely on the pillars of innovation, investment in R&D, and staying one step ahead of the competition.

Ability The executives were uncovered as the key part, enveloping the specialty of drawing in and holding top ability and sustaining administration for hierarchical progression. A flourishing hierarchical culture, where ability isn't recently overseen but decisively developed, arose as the mystery ingredient for supported achievement.

In the domain of monetary wellness, we uncovered the standards of judicious monetary administration, guaranteeing sound income, and enhancing costs for proficiency. The capacity to explore monetary intricacies with shrewdness and foreknowledge turned into a demonstration of an association's strength and key ability.

Organizations and collaborations turned into the essential gas pedals, with the investigation of associations, joint efforts for shared development, and getting to new business sectors and advancements filling in as doors to undiscovered possibility. The force of cooperation arose as a power that moves individual associations forward as well as lifts whole enterprises.

As we conclude this excursion, it's urgent to underscore that the experiences and procedures introduced are not only hypothetical developments. They are the synthesis of knowledge gleaned from successful practices, real-world experiences, and the collective wisdom of business leaders who have triumphed over adversity.

In the powerful universe of business, achievement isn't an objective but rather a constant excursion of variation, development, and key development. As a senior chief, you hold the light to enlighten this way for your association. Outfitted with the information and techniques introduced in this aide, you are not only a latent eyewitness to progress but rather a proactive modeler of a future where development exceeds all logical limitations.

This is your aide, your compass, and your essential playbook. May it engage you to lead with strength, enhance with intensity, and shape a future where your association flourishes in the midst of difficulties, adjusts to open doors, and accomplishes extraordinary development and greatness.